BICYCLING CALIFORNIA'S SPINE:

TOURING THE LENGTH OF THE SIERRA NEVADA

Written, photographed
and designed
by
Bil Paul

A Bikeroots Edition

*All rights reserved. No part of this work
may be reproduced or transmitted in any
form or by any means, or by any information
storage or retrieval system without
permission in writing from the publisher.*

PUBLISHED BY ALCHEMIST/LIGHT PUBLISHING
Box 5530   San Francisco   California   94101

ISBN: 0-9600650-3-2
Library of Congress Cat. Card: 80-70010

Copyright © 1981 by Bil Paul

Climbing Luther Pass.

- CONTENTS -

INTRODUCTION	4
PARTICULARS	6
MAP SYMBOLS	9
WHAT--AND HOW--TO PACK	10
DAY-BY-DAY GUIDE AND ACCOUNTS	
Day 1. NW entrance Lassen Volcanic National Park to Chester, CA	12
Day 2. Chester, CA, to Quincy, CA	16
Day 3. Quincy, CA, to Cottonwood Campground near Sierraville, CA	18
Day 4. Cottonwood Campground to Kaspian Rec. Area, Lake Tahoe	22
Day 5. Kaspian Recreation Area to South Lake Tahoe, CA	24
Day 6. South Lake Tahoe, CA, to Walker, CA	28
Day 7. Walker, CA, to Lee Vining, CA	30
Day 8. Lee Vining, CA, to White Wolf Campground, Yosemite Nat. Park	34
Day 9. White Wolf Campground to Mariposa, CA	36
Day 10. Mariposa, CA, to Spring Cove Campground at Bass Lake	40
Day 11. Spring Cove Campground to Dora Belle Campground, Shaver Lake	42
Day 12. Dora Belle Campground to Camp $4\frac{1}{2}$ near Pine Flat Lake	46
Day 13. Camp $4\frac{1}{2}$ to General Grant Grove, Kings Canyon National Park	48
Day 14. General Grant Grove to Three Rivers, CA	52
Day 15. Three Rivers, CA, to Camp Nelson, CA	54
Day 16. Camp Nelson to Kernville, CA	56
OTHER SIERRA BIKERS	58
PRODUCT EVALUATIONS	60
RESOURCES	62

-INTRODUCTION-

I decided to find another north-south long-distance bike route in California as an alternative to the popular coastal bike route--here you have it. I chose a Sierra route over other possibilities because of its varied scenery, cooler high-altitude temperatures, abundance of parks and facilities, and numerous roads and passes.

* * *

One of the fascinations with California is that so much diversity is packed within the borders of one state. California has southern deserts and a cool, rainy section along the north Pacific coast. In the state's midsection, a great flat central agricultural valley (hot in the summer) is enclosed by two long mountain ranges. These ranges part ways in the north near the quiet Mt. Shasta and Mt. Lassen volcanoes and run parallel to each other (refer to the map on the rear cover) until meeting south of Bakersfield. The western chain is the Coastal Range; its peaks run from 2,000 to 8,000 feet (600 to 2,400 m) high. The eastern range, the proud "spine" of California, is 400-500 miles long, has an average width of 70 miles, and has peaks in the 7,000 to 15,000 foot (2,100 to 4,500 m) category. This Sierra Nevada, or "Snowy Range", has a gradually ascending western slope and a sharply dropping eastern side.

Technically, the Sierra Nevada begins at the North Fork of the Feather River and ends at Tejon Pass in the south. The route I offer here doesn't follow this definition religiously, because I wanted to include Mt. Lassen park to the north and because mountain roads south of Lake Isabella are practically nonexistant. My wife and I drove the projected route in August, 1980, and I bicycled most of it the next month. I was unable to bicycle the Day 1 portion (Mt. Lassen park) because the road was temporarily snowed in and the Day 15 and 16 portions (Three Rivers to Lake Isabella) because of ninety-degree heat in the lower altitudes. For those two portions I rely on our auto notes and on maps. Additionally, I didn't take side trips all the way into Yosemite Valley or into Kings Canyon because I'd spent time in those areas before and wanted to preserve the momentum of my journey. But I offer maps of those areas for those who'd like to linger and explore.

Those cyclists who might wish to do a portion of my route will find this book a help (in my opinion, the portion of the route from Mt. Lassen through Yosemite is the best) as will folks who would just like to read about mountain touring and experiences.

Every seasoned bicycle tourist has his or her individual style of travelling. My own particular style is a combination of roughing it and rewarding myself. On this trip, I generally ate a good self-made (cold) breakfast, snacked during the day, ate heavily at restaurants at night, and camped in campgrounds (no lack of them in the Sierra). About every fourth day I'd stay in a motel. Using this system, I spent about $15 per day. Other cyclists like to totally camp out and cook; sometimes a budget makes the determination.

*　　　　*　　　　*

This book would not have been possible without the help of my wife Lorraine, who drove many miles with me and helped take notes, then lived with my many hours at the typewriter. Finally, she proofread the manuscript. Thanks also go to Peter Peabody, who biked many miles with me when I was getting in shape for the big one.

If you do some touring in the Sierra Nevada I'd like to hear from you about your experiences--if this book is revised I will try to include any new pertinent information. Also let me know if I've made any errors. Write me care of Alchemist/Light Publishing. Good cycling to you!

Bill Paul

ABOVE: altitude profile for the entire route I used. Tick marks on the top indicate days of travel. Beyond Yosemite, the dramatic altitude changes are caused by a lack of through mountain roads that necessitates dips into the foothills.

-PARTICULARS-

Several things separate alpine (read Sierra) touring from near-sea level touring. First, the hills are bigger. Second, the air is thinner. Third, the weather can be more freakish and harsh.

Considering the bigger "hills", two suggestions are in order. One is that you're going to have to be in darn good shape. Think in terms of gaining 4,000 or 5,000 feet (1200 or 1500 m) in one day of riding. For this trip I rode 400 miles previously to get in shape, including workouts over the toughest terrain I could find. Ride every hill in your vicinity. The other suggestion is to have some very low gearing on your machine. I had my Univega 15-speed outfitted to go as low as 29 inches and would've gone lower had I been able to.

Altitudes on the entirety of this route vary from 800 feet (240 m) to 10,000 feet (3,000 m). It's hard to say just when and where one would notice the effects of thin air on bicycle riding--it depends upon the level of exertion and the altitude. The problem is that in thinner air the body can't move enough oxygen to the muscles. The cyclist finds himself breathing heavier and getting tired more easily. By working out and training at high altitudes, one's body will tend to acclimate itself to the change in environment.

Along with less oxygen, the thinner air also has less water vapor, making dry skin a problem. Taking skin moisturizing cream along is a good idea. The sun (especially ultraviolet light) is stronger because there's less air to stop it. A good sun lotion or cream (I used a number 6) will keep sunburn at bay and still enable the cyclist to get a sexy tan. Lip balm or screen and sunglasses are a good idea.

The thing to really prepare for on any Sierra trip is the weather. Temperature extremes are the norm. In sunny weather, high altitude daytime temperatures climb up into the 70's to 90's (F^o, summertime) depending upon the altitude. But at night, temperatures can plunge into the 40's (near $0^o C$) and down below freezing. Someone calculated that every 1,000-foot (300-m) gain in altitude is equivalent to moving 300 miles (500 km) north or a $2-3^o F$ drop in temperature. Freakish storms can and do occur in the Sierra. Snow in June or September (or even in the months between) is possible. After the lower mountains of the Coastal Range, the Sierra Nevada is the second and higher obstacle to the passage of Pacific Ocean storms. The Sierra tends to get dumped on; much of California's water and hydroelectric power comes from the tremendous amount of snow that accumulates after winter storms. In the summer, clouds can form over the mountains and release rain while the rest of the state remains sunny and dry.

As far as winds go, I found them tricky and fickle in the Sierra. They tend to follow the canyons, going up them during the day as the warm valley air rises. Unlike my earlier Mississippi River trip, winds weren't much of an impediment on this trip.

Below find temperature and precipitation data for a weather station in Blue Canyon, at the 5,000-foot (1,500-m) level in the Sierra Nevada, not far from Lake Tahoe. For comparison purposes, I've included a temperature graph for the valley city of Fresno. If you've never read one of these graphs before, it may take a minute or two to get the grasp of it:

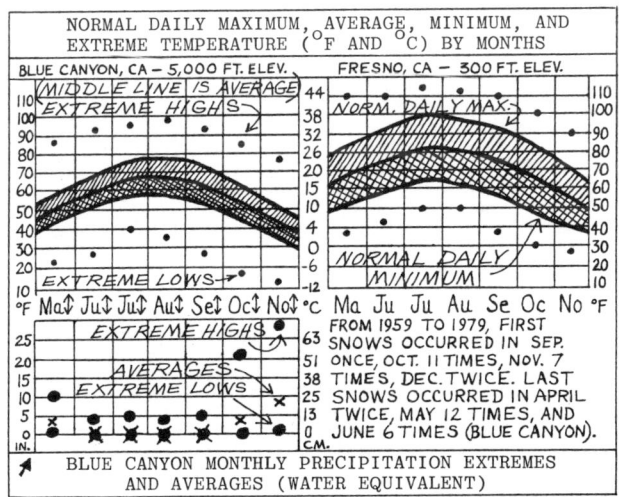

The alpine tourist must be prepared for extremes. He
or she has the advantage of being on roads rather
than on remote trails. But I still recommend taking
a tent, rain gear, and cold weather gear. People have
died from exposure and hypothermia in the summer at
the 5,000-foot level because all they had with them
when it snowed was light summer clothing. The idea in
cold, snowy conditions is to get to lower altitudes
or shelter, to stay dry, and to keep moving. Never
keep pushing on in the face of impossible condi-
tions--hitch a ride if need be and swallow your
pride. I cut my trip short when faced with too much
heat. That brings up the other extreme--heat exhaus-
tion, brought about by the body losing too much
water. The treatment is to lie down and drink some
liquids. Always take more water than you think you'll
need (see Day 13). Listen to weather reports on a
radio and know what's in the offing. Watch your body
signs, don't overdo, and rest often.

The best months to travel the Sierra are probably
September and October. The rain and snow season in
California lasts from November through April. The
Sierra could be biked from June through August,
though some of the passes could still be snowed in
during June. The main problem in the summer is heat
and vacation traffic; both are down in the fall.

The matter of riding safety. On my trip I had no
close calls, despite the many logging trucks on the
roads. For visibility, I used a Cycle Guard tri-
angular flag, and, the few times I rode at night, a
Belt Beacon. I recommend both. But I'd like to dis-
courage night riding in the mountains, period--too
dangerous on the winding, up and down roads. At any
time of the day it's wise to use high-visibility
light-colored clothing and bike packs. Use a helmet
and try out a rear-view mirror. It's important to
start a Sierra tour with new, properly-adjusted
brake pads and cables. Before long downhills, test
them. On the descent (some last a half hour or more)
intermittent braking is preferable to constant
braking so as not to overheat wheel rims and damage
tires and tubes. Stop once in awhile and let your
rims cool--having a flat on a downhill means losing
steering control.

Certain campgrounds along this route require Ticketron reservations during peak times of the year--
a way to deal with overcrowding. For national parks,
the following campgrounds in Yosemite Valley require
reservations from Memorial Day (early May) to Labor
Day (early Sept.): North Pine, Upper and Lower Pines,

and Upper and Lower River. For the same period, add Lodgepole Campground in Sequoia Park. It's best to visit a Ticketron agency in person (they charge a $1.75 fee for the transaction), or, if you're not near one, write Ticketron, PO Box 26430, San Francisco, CA 94126. Reservations can be made up to 8 weeks in advance. Forest Service campsites along this route which require reservations are all 5 around Bass Lake (see Day 10) from May 22-Sept. 11, and, in the Lake Tahoe area, Fallen Leaf (June 13-Sept. 11), Nevada Beach (June 13-Sept. 11), and Meeks Bay (Aug. 1-Sept. 11). Visit Ticketron or write for a Ticketron reservation form from the Forest Service, 630 Sansome St., San Francisco, CA 94111. State parks along this route which require reservations are D.L. Bliss and Emerald Bay in the Tahoe area (both June 22-Sept. 3) and Grover Hot Springs near Markleeville (May 19-Sept. 17). For a state park reservation, visit Ticketron or request a Ticketron reservation form from the Dept. of Parks and Recreation, PO Box 2390, Sacramento, CA 95811. Other campgrounds (and the above campgrounds outside the reservation periods) are operated on a first-come, first-served basis. If you arrive at a camping area and there aren't any sites open, look for a site with just a few people and ask if you can share--it works.

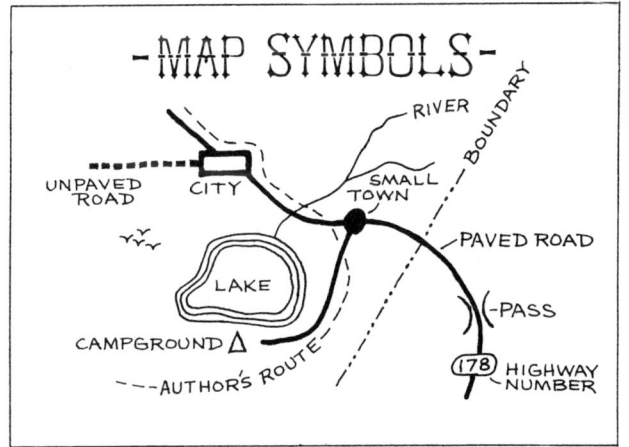

-WHAT-AND HOW-TO PACK-

Here is how I packed my bike, what I took (and a few things I forgot), and how much the whole thing weighed. Other than the cold weather clothing and items designated optional (*), these items might be carried on any type of touring. Many of these items never get used, but part of the fun of touring is being <u>compleat</u>. Travelling in a group could cut down on weight--one person could carry the tools, one the tent, etc.

TOOL KIT--3 lb.: pliers; phillips and regular screwdriver; crescent wrench; crank removal tool; chain link tool; spoke tool; cone wrench; freewheel removal tool; hex key (allen) wrenches; third hand brake tool*; 2 tire irons; spare brake pads; spare inner tube; tire pressure gauge; tube patch kit; matching spare spokes; spare wheel bearings; 2 derailleur cables; 2 brake cables; "gaffer" or "duct" tape (for tire repair)*; bearing grease; light oil or Tri-flon; wire (for misc. repairs); large cleaning rag; cleaning toothbrush; extra nuts, bolts, and washers; and a tool bag (attaches to rear of seat).

CAMPING (ETC.) MODULE--16 lb.: nylon pup tent (with netting and floor), sleeping bag, ensolite pad, rain poncho, and waterproof stuff bag to hold items. Lashed to top of module: long windbreaker, cotton zip sweater, and long riding trousers.

PANNIERS--10 lb.: spare tire; knit wool hat; insulated waterproof gloves; swim suit*; 1 pair heavy, warm socks; 3 pair regular socks; 3 T-shirts; 2 briefs; 1 long-sleeved thermal underwear top; 1 long-sleeved cotton shirt*; toilet paper; razor*; shaving soap*, shampoo; soap; washcloth; small towel; comb; toothbrush; jackknife and spoon; suntan cream; lip balm or screen; skin moisturizer; matches in waterproof container; mosquito repellent; mosquito netting to cover head*; breakfast food; emergency package of freeze-dried food; baking soda (for brushing teeth); talcum powder (for chafed skin); miniature can opener; sewing kit; vitamins; water purifications tablets; first aid kit (include poison oak and chigger medicine and whistle).

HANDLEBAR PACK--8 lb.: arm light, radio, extra batteries, extra bulbs, compass, sunglasses (also keeps bugs out of eyes), sweat band (keeps sweat out of sunglasses), rear-view mirror* (attaches to sunglasses), snacks, plastic eating bowl, watch, maps, cuff clips, notebook and pen*, books*, photo gear*, and film*.

KNAPSACK*--11 lb. (not the best place to carry weight): 35mm camera with case*, telephoto lens*, wallet, and traveller's checks.

BELL PRIME HELMET--1 lb.

TWO FULL WATER BOTTLES PLUS ZEFAL AIR PUMP--3 lb.

UNIVEGA 27" GRAN TURISMO BIKE--33 lb., with: lock and cable, plastic fenders (a must for wet weather riding), Blackburn rack with rear-mounted Belt Beacon*, Cycle Guard traffic clearance flag*, Huret odometer*, Schwinn Le Tour tires, and puncture resistant tubes. Gearing: 36-47-52/14-17-21-28-34.

SOME CALCULATIONS:

Weight of bike & access.	33 lb. (12+%)
Weight of packs/gear	52 lb. (19+%)
Author's weight	185 lb. (68+%)
	270 lb. (100%)

Many tourists worry about having too much weight over the rear wheel. I calculated that when I rode the Univega without packs and with hands on the lower handlebars, the rear wheel bore 63% of the total weight. With the extra 52 lbs. of packs and gear (mostly on the rear) and with hands on the lower handlebars, the rear wheel bore only 64% of the weight. This surprised me; sometimes we forget that the rider's weight is the main consideration. Putting a lot of weight on the front can make steering sluggish.

DAY 1

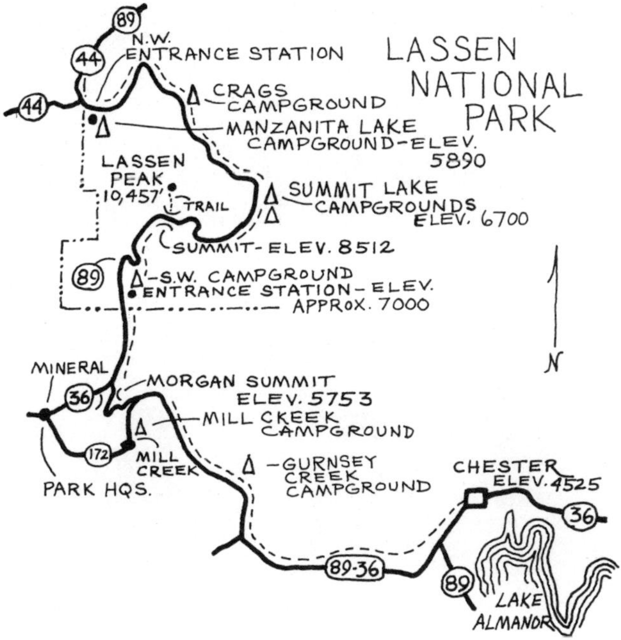

LASSEN NATIONAL PARK

- N.W. Entrance Station (89/44)
- Crags Campground
- Manzanita Lake Campground — Elev. 5890
- Lassen Peak 10,457 — Trail
- Summit Lake Campgrounds — Elev. 6700
- Summit — Elev. 8512
- S.W. Campground Entrance Station — Elev. approx. 7000
- Mineral (36)
- Morgan Summit — Elev. 5753
- Mill Creek Campground
- Park HQS. (172) — Mill Creek
- Gurnsey Creek Campground
- Chester — Elev. 4525 (36)
- 89·36 / 89 — Lake Almanor

N ↑

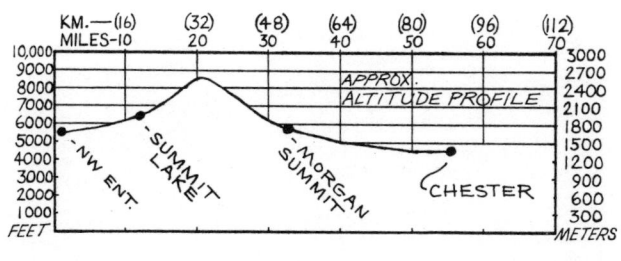

Approx. Altitude Profile — NW Ent., Summit Lake, Morgan Summit, Chester

12

DAY 1. NW ENTRANCE LASSEN VOLCANIC NATIONAL PARK TO CHESTER, CA. 56 miles (90 km). Circling a recently active volcano.

This portion was checked out by car and from other sources because the park road was temporarily snowed in and impossible to cycle in mid-September 1980 (see photo next page). Even in August, when we drove through, there was some off-road snow at 8,000 feet (2400 m).

It is possible to start this trip by taking an AMTRAK Coast Starlight train to Redding, CA. At this time, AMTRAK requires that bikes be boxed. If you box the bike yourself, there is no extra charge for taking a bike along. Some of the larger train stations (San Francisco and Los Angeles for example) have boxes for sale at $4. There is an AMTRAK connection at the southern end of this route, at Bakersfield, but it is not possible to take a bike aboard the train there. From Redding, it's a 47-mile (75 km) ride on Hwy. 44 and a gradual altitude gain of 5,000 feet (1500 m) to the northwest entrance to Lassen Park. There are several small towns with stores along the way.

Mt. Lassen, at the southern end of the Cascade Range, last erupted in 1914 and volcanic activity continued for 7 years. Steam vents are still active at some places along the 30-mile (48 km) park road, which is on the narrow side. At 8 miles or 13 km from the NW entrance, a 2½ mile or 4 km hiking trail leaves the park road and makes its way to the crater at the top of Mt. Lassen--a 3- to 5-hour round trip.

Near the NW entrance station is Manzanita Lake Campground, the largest in the park with 179 sites and a small store. Down the road 4 miles or 6 km is Crags Campground with 45 sites. Eight miles or 13 km beyond is Summit Lake Campground with 94 sites. Near the SW entrance station is Southwest Campground (naturally) with 21 campsites and reportedly a store. The Lassen campgrounds are open approximately from mid-June through September 15, depending on snow and usage. It should be noted that Lassen park is not as well-known as the other national parks on this route and consequently isn't as crowded. Outside the park, Mill Creek Campground (small) and Gurnsey Creek Campground (see map) are open from May 1st through the end of October. Chester is a fair-sized city with motels, restaurants, a hospital and (it is said) a bike shop. My wife and I ate at the Bear Club restaurant--medium prices for large food portions. We stayed at the Sierra Motel in Chester ($20).

Above: unseasonal snow covering Mt. Lassen on September 13, 1980. Below: the author at Manzanita Lake Campground, shivering in the cold, after finding the park road snowed in.

Above: migrating Canada geese near Lake Almanor. Below: thistle-seed-eating Goldfinch along the roadside near Graeagle. A 400mm lens was used for both photographs.

DAY 2

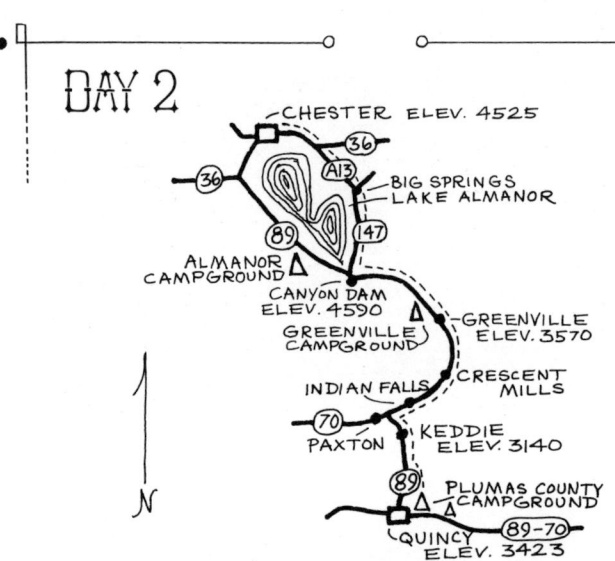

DAY 2. CHESTER, CA, TO QUINCY, CA. 46.5 miles (74 km). Mostly downhill and easy. Take the wide, broad-shouldered Hwy. 36 east from Chester--I saw hundreds of migrating Canadian geese feeding on the lake flats there in September. After 5 miles, turn right on the equally-wide Hwy. A13. Four miles beyond, turn right again onto Hwy. 147. After 7 more miles of riding along the picturesque lakefront, dotted by docks, homes, and resorts, you'll arrive at the intersection with Hwy. 89. The Hwy. 147 route is said to be prettier than the Hwy. 89 route down the west side of the lake. A campground (Almanor) is 9 miles or 15 km south of Chester, just off that

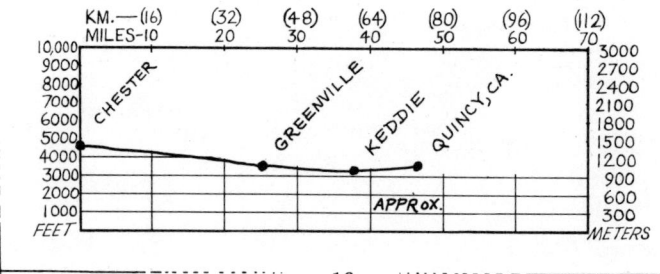

stretch of Hwy. 89. It reportedly has groceries and swimming and is open from June through September.

As the elevation profile indicates, today's ride is hardly stressful. From Canyon Dam, the ride is all downhill until the Hwy. 70-89 junction. From the Hwy. 147-89 junction, it's 9 miles or 15 km to Greenville, which has a number of stores and is the largest town between Chester and Quincy--I made my lunch stop there. Two miles north of Greenville on 89 is a campground run by the county with 16 sites (no fee). After Greenville, follow Hwy. 89 12 miles or 19 km down a beautiful river canyon to the Hwy. 89-70 junction. Turn left on 89 and proceed uphill past a spring where you may want to stop for a drink. Ten miles or 16 km from the intersection is the city of Quincy, a metropolis of 5,000 souls nestled in the flats of a mountain valley.

I stayed at the Plumas County Campground, adjacent to the county fairgrounds (where stock car races were in progress). To get there, bike about a mile east of the Quincy city center on Hwy. 89/70, turn left at Plumas-Fairgrounds Rd., then ride one-fourth mile. The fee of $2 wasn't collected. One complaint: the toilets were all backed up and inoperable. Another campground which I didn't check out is the Quincy Campground, operated by the Forest Service. It's one-fourth mile beyond the first campground on 89--turn left on County Road E19 and ride a quarter-mile. This area may be superior--it reportedly has a grocery and laundry ($2 fee; open from May through mid-October).

I ate at the Mountain House restaurant on the business strip along 89/70 near the campgrounds (motels there). Mountain House is your basic-burger place with extras like salads and deserts. The food was OK. An attraction was that the place had large windows so that I could keep an eye on my bike and gear outside. My procedure is usually to set up my tent to hold down a camping site, then keep the rest of the gear on my bike till I'm ready to return and settle down for the night. Then I take all the packs off the bike and put them in the tent.

I saw many pickups on the road loaded down with firewood--September seemed to be the time of the year for stocking up.

DAY 3

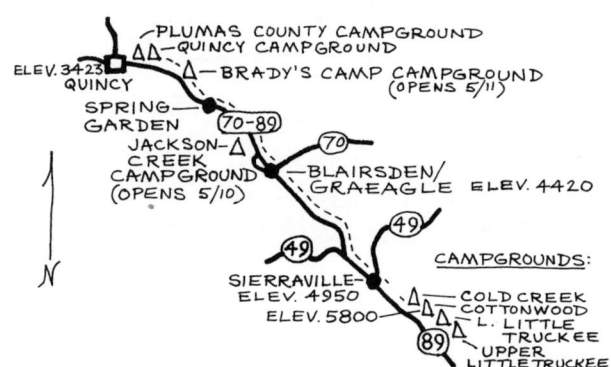

DAY 3. QUINCY, CA, TO COTTONWOOD CAMPGROUND NEAR SIERRAVILLE, CA. 48 miles (77 km). Some nice country.
Approximately 5 miles (8 km) east of Quincy is a rest area with bathrooms, water, and a phone. After this point, there is a bike lane of sorts. Eight miles (13 km) from Quincy is the tiny town of Spring Garden, population 80, with a country store and post office. There are quite a few logging trucks on Hwy. 89 in this area. In September the days were heating up fast; I found that I wore my long trousers only a short time before stripping to my riding shorts. Fourteen miles (35 km) from Quincy is the little town of Sloat, off the highway. No stores; mainly a sawmill operation. At this point I tried an off-the-highway road which meets Hwy. 89/70 again near Cromwell. Don't take it! The paved road degenerated into a rocky, torturous little dirt road, which turned

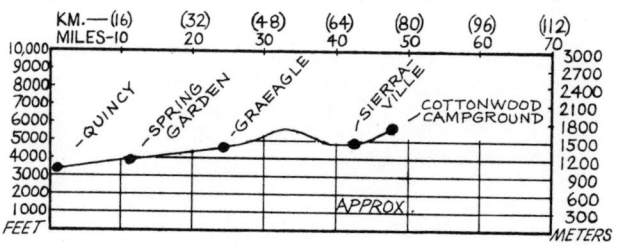

into many little roads and had me cussing and cursing my luck.

Jackson Creek Campground, near Cromwell, has 15 sites. Down the road a ways, before reaching the 3 close-together towns of Mohawk, Blairsden and Graeagle (try to spell that one) is Little Bear Campground, a private place with showers and swimming ($6 per site). Turn right on Little Bear Rd. to find it. Just after that, on 89, turn right at the Mohawk Ranger Station (I used the rest rooms there) and ride across the old bridge (people swim under it during the summer) to an intersection. Turn left and proceed into Mohawk where there's a 9-5 pm Mohawk Resort Smorgasbord. Follow the main road on into Graeagle, a recreation-type area with a golf course and a lot of old folks. This is a good place for a midday rest stop.

After Graeagle, Hwy. 89 is nice and meandering, with close-in trees and shade. In the vicinity of the Plumas-Sierra county line there's a long uphill pull, with the summit pegged at 5441 feet (1632 m). After coasting to the bottom, Sierraville is 8 miles (13 km) away, across a broad, flat valley. I ate in the Stage Stop Restaurant there and watched the constant stream of huge truck rigs pass by while I savored my big spaghetti dinner ($6.85 with extras).

It's another uphill pull--an altitude gain of about 1,000 feet (300 m)--to the campgrounds on Hwy. 89 above Sierraville. The first two, Cold Creek (small, but along a stream) and Cottonwood (large) are 5 miles or 8 km from Sierraville. Seven miles or 11 km beyond are Upper and Lower Little Truckee Campgrounds. All are open from approximately mid-June through October.

I pulled into Cottonwood Campground and set up camp just as darkness came on--I barely had enough time to get a fire going. I remembered the incident earlier in the day when the driver of a camper passing me inexplicably yelled out, "BASTARD!" Wondering about his motivation had given me something to think about for quite a few miles. The fee at Cottonwood (which was almost deserted) was $2. Payment was voluntary--no one ever came around to collect money at any federally-operated campground on my whole trip.

Above: stock-car racing at Plumas County Fairgrounds in Quincy. Below: checking the morning mail at the Spring Garden contract post office, one the Postal Service would like to close down. The town has a population of 80.

Along the main street in Truckee. Many shops and eateries to check out; a pleasant stopping place.

DAY 4

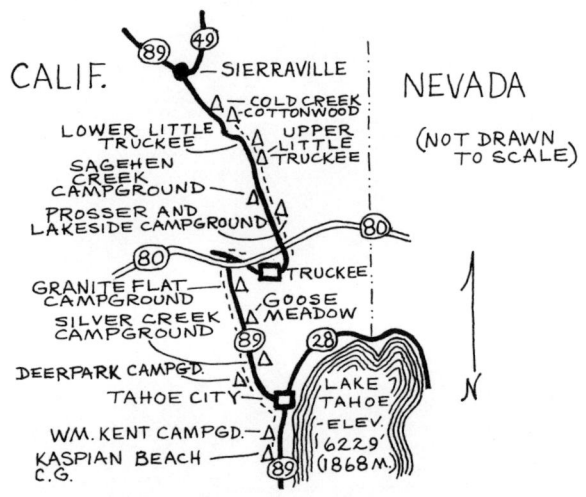

DAY 4. COTTONWOOD CAMPGROUND TO KASPIAN RECREATION AREA, LAKE TAHOE. 40 miles (64 km). Reaching the jewel of the Sierras. From Cottonwood, it's 7 miles or 11 km on Hwy. 89 south to the 2 Little Truckee Campgrounds and 15 miles or 24 km to the Prosser Lake campgrounds. The terrain is not difficult with some moderate hills. Before arriving at Truckee (21 mi. or 32 km from Cottonwood), Hwy. 89 passes the site where the Donner Party was stranded with their wagon train by 1846 snows with the loss of

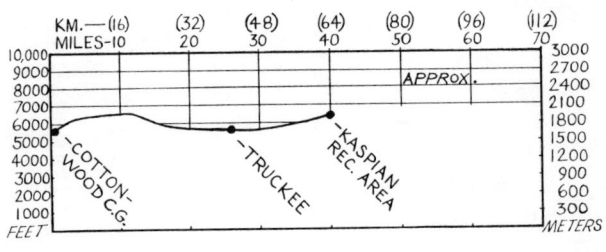

many lives. Donner Pass is named for them. A few
years later, in 1849, 40,000 "49-ers" used the pass
on their way to California gold fields or settlement.

When crossing over Interstate Highway 80, a sign
says you're on Hwy. 267. Follow the road but continue
straight on the main street in Truckee instead
of turning left on 267 at the town's edge. Hwy. 89 is
a much better route to Tahoe than 267. Truckee is an
alive, fairly hip little city where I made my midday
stop and actually met a couple who'd bought my first
guidebook. Truckee has considerable tourist trade,
being on the way from I-80 to Tahoe. After you've
visited in town continue on Donner Pass Rd. through
a business section for 3/4 mile, then turn left at
a Safeway store. Head south on this road, under I-80
again, and you are on good old 89 once more. The portion
of this highway from Truckee to the Squaw
Valley turnoff is absolutely beautiful--wide, with a
bike lane and gradual gradient in a scenic valley
that makes biking a real pleasure. 1½ mile or 2½ km
from I-80 is Granite Flat Campground; 5 miles from
I-80 is Goose Meadow Campground (both camps don't
provide piped water--some people told me they were
getting their water from the fast-flowing, nearby
Truckee River). Eight miles or 12 km from I-80 is
Silver Creek Campground with piped water ($2 fee).
About 1 mile south of the Squaw Valley turnoff is
Deerpark Campground with no piped water.

Hwy. 89 narrows after Deerpark, but fortunately a
short distance later a well-kept, paved bike path
begins and runs into Tahoe City. In Tahoe City turn
right onto West Lake Blvd. (also Hwy. 89) and head
south on the bike path. Be warned: during the temperate
months, the west shore of Tahoe is busy.
After having pedalled for several days in the open
countryside with not much traffic I suddenly felt
transported into a major city.

Two miles south of Tahoe City, the William Kent
Campground hoves into view. A few miles beyond, I
was allowed to camp in an unmarked camping area on
a hill behind the Kaspian Beach parking area. I was
the only one there; lonely. Next to the parking lot
is a small building with toilets and washbasins.

I ate at Clemintine's restaurant approximately 1
mile north of Kaspian--a higher-priced place but I
felt in an expansive mood upon having reached such
an urbane locale. $10.35 for a big, delicious meal.

DAY 5

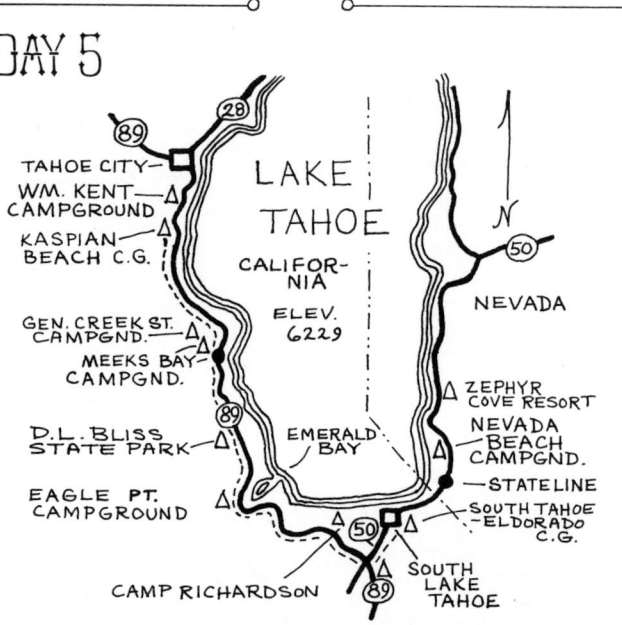

<u>DAY 5. KASPIAN RECREATION AREA TO SOUTH LAKE TAHOE, CA. 23 miles (37 km). Some extra time; views of a great lake.</u> This leg of the tour is purposefully short so as to have some time to spend in South Lake Tahoe and Stateline, for those who might wish to gamble, sightsee, rest, or stock up on goodies. South Lake Tahoe/Stateline is the largest population center and shopping area on the lake. Lake Tahoe itself is 22 miles or 36 km long, 10 miles or 16 km wide, and reaches a depth of 650 feet (195 m). One could ride all around the lake in a good day's jaunt of 72 miles or 116 km.

I'll cover the west- and south-lake campgrounds. Because Tahoe is a tourist mecca, they might be crowded in the summer months and reservations may be necessary. Heading south from Kaspian, General Creek State Campground (part of Sugar Pine Pt. State Park) is 1 mile south of Tahoma. It has showers in the summer. $5 per day, Ticketron reservations. Next is Meeks Bay Campground at the town of Meeks Bay. It's a Forest Service campground with a $3 fee and is near the beach. Ticketron reservations. D.L.

Bliss State Park is 10 miles or 16 km north of South Lake Tahoe. Ticketron reservations. Eagle Point Campground above Emerald Bay is 8 miles or 13 km north of South Lake Tahoe on Hwy. 89. Ticketron reservations. Camp Richardson is a private campground 2½ miles north of the Hwy. 89/50 junction, on Hwy. 89 (showers, tent camping, and cabins--a $5 minimum). For a campground that isn't shown on some maps, take Fallen Leaf Road about a mile south from 89 and the Camp Richardson area to Fallen Leaf Campground (Forest Service; Ticketron reservations). A caution: people camping in unauthorized places on beaches can find themselves in trouble with the law, or so I heard. Another private campground is the Tahoe Valley Recreational Campground ½ mile south of the 89/50 intersection on Hwy. 89. Turn left on 'C' St. and go one block (showers, $7.50 per day for a tent, open all year). The South Tahoe-Eldorado Campground is located in South Lake Tahoe (the city) where Lake Tahoe Blvd. (Hwy. 50) abruptly meets the lake. May be the most crowded of all (showers, reservations recommended). In Nevada, Nevada Beach Campground (Forest Service) is $3 per day. Ticketron reservations. North of Nevada Beach, Zephyr Cove Resort has a private campground ($4 per day, open all year, reservations suggested).

An elevation profile is not included today because most of the riding is at lake level. The exception is the long uphill that begins at Bliss State Park and takes the cyclist several hundred feet above Emerald Bay--a stunning view. The downhill is steep with switchbacks that require considerable braking. Soon after reaching the flats, a bike path begins that parallels Hwy. 89 into South Lake Tahoe. Nice.

I stayed in the relatively inexpensive El Nido motel on the Hwy. 50 business strip heading into South Lake Tahoe from the Hwy. 89/50 junction. Many motels in the area. The El Nido has a pool and jacuzzi. I scored a lot of food for myself at the all-you-can-eat buffet at the Sahara Tahoe Casino in Stateline, Nevada ($4.50). All the casinos are clustered just across the state border in Nevada where gambling is legal. A trip to Tahoe wouldn't be complete without at least looking at the gambling--it's an unreal world. Also, there might be some entertainment you'd want to see. Motels give out discount coupons and free buses stop to take people and their wallets to the gambling joints. I always keep my bike in my motel room.

These trucks, familiar in mountain areas, haul 30 to 35 tons of logs--and cyclists share the road with them. The driver above said he bicycles and motorcycles himself and takes care when passing cyclists. A few truckers, he admitted, are not so considerate (their attitude: "Bicyclists have to be crazy to be up here."). The point is, never press an idealogical point with a logging truck--trucks of this weight speed downhill so as to gain momentum for the next grade and it's much easier for a cyclist to stop than one of them. Also, rig drivers are prevented by high fenders from getting a good view of cyclists they pass. This driver recommended not cycling at night, getting off the road when taking pictures, and not roadhogging by riding side by side as some bike groups are prone to do. He said some roads are barely wide enough for 2 trucks!

Above: Lake Tahoe. Below: playing the casino slot machines in Stateline, Nevada, near the lake.

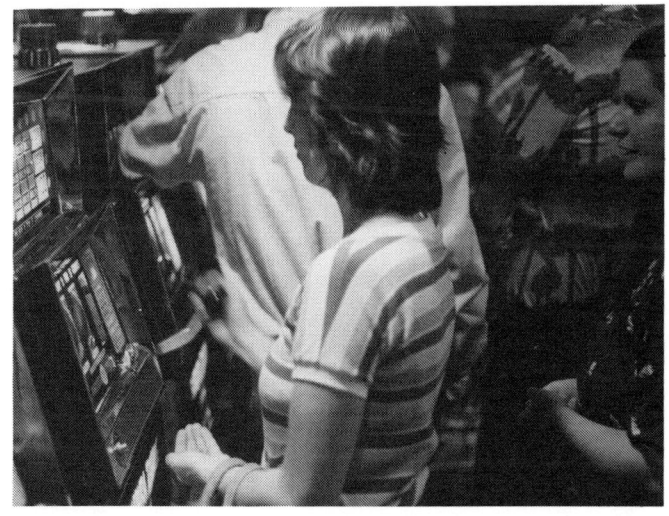

DAY 6

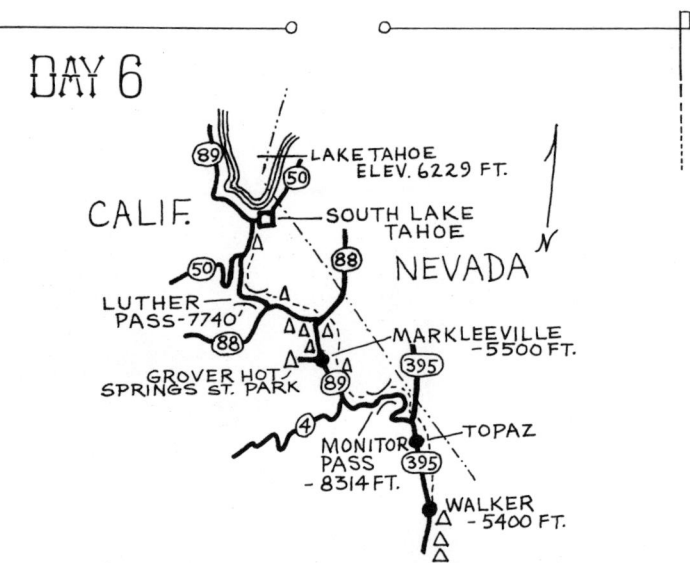

DAY 6. SOUTH LAKE TAHOE, CA, TO WALKER, CA. 63 miles (100 km). Joining the mountain goats. The altitude profile says it all: today begins some challenging climbing that the previous 5 days could be considered training for. Today's ride of 63 miles, over Luther and Monitor Passes, is a long one. Because of the campgrounds between the two, it's possible to cut this trip in half.

From the Hwy. 89/50 junction near South Lake Tahoe, it's 5 miles along a business strip (a KOA campground here, fee about $8) to the point where 89 departs 50 and heads upward toward Luther Pass. Be-

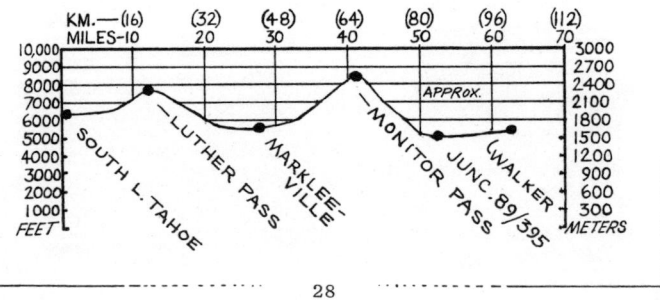

yond Luther Pass is the broad, beautiful Hope Valley, where I met a pair of touring cyclists. At the end of the valley is the Hope Valley Store; after it, across a bridge, is a long downhill through a strikingly beautiful canyon with a number of campgrounds, some near a sparkling mountain stream: Kit Carson, Snowshoe Springs, and Crystal Springs ($3 each, Forest Service). Down out of the canyon, on more level territory, there's Turtle Rock County Park ($3), where my wife and I stayed overnight during our car trip (a nice place) and Indian Creek Reservoir Campground (off the highway a ways). Markleeville, 28 miles or 45 km from South Lake Tahoe, has a store and is the jumping-off place for Grover Hot Springs State Park (4 miles off Hwy. 89)--a very popular place--reservations required. Markleeville, incidentally, is the county seat of Alpine County, the least populated of California's counties with only 900 citizens. Every once in awhile an organization gets the idea that if they just moved 900 settlers in, they could take over the county and have their own little paradise. One mile beyond Markleeville is Markleeville Campground with 10 sites and water (Forest Service). From there to the 89/4 junction the going is rather level--the climb begins afterwards. This eastern side of the Sierra is dry, with sparse vegetation--most of the rain and snow lands on the western side. On the climb up to Monitor Pass I stopped and rested a good deal.

Monitor Pass itself isn't a dramatic summit but is rather on the end of a flat, breezy and lonely plateau. The 8% gradient downhill afterwards is serpentine, with a great view. Just before hitting Hwy. 395, you'll pass down a narrow and quite beautiful canyon. Turn right on 395 and ride the flats to the little towns of Topaz (has a store) and Coleville. Riding this stretch, I ran into some swarms of bugs that were so thick I felt like I was being rained on (sunglasses kept them out of my eyes). Between the two towns I had to hitch a ride on a pickup because of road work. I camped overnight in Walker (pop. 300) in the privately-run Buckskin Campground ($2.50; has showers and a washing machine) and ate at the Basque Restaurant (family style with salad bar--$9.43 with tip). Four miles south of Walker along 395 is Shingle Mill Flat Campground; 4 miles beyond are Bootleg and Chris Flat Campgrounds. During the night at Buckskin Campground something (or someone) took a leak on my tent, just above my head. Now, that's incredible.

DAY 7

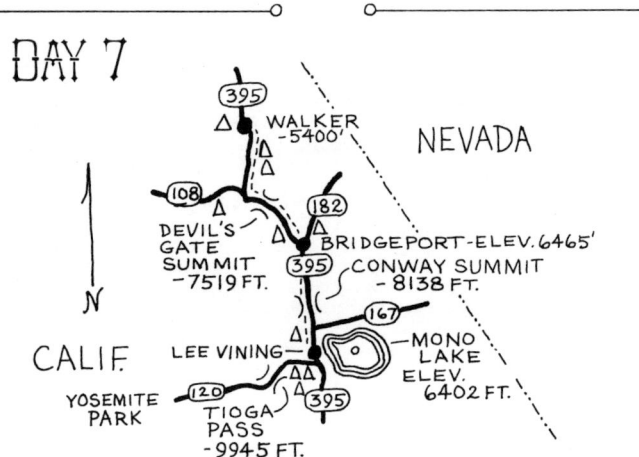

DAY 7. WALKER, CA, TO LEE VINING, CA. 57 miles (90 km). More climbing; an unusual lake. The campgrounds just beyond Walker are covered in Day 6; in September trout fishermen were occupying them. There were also some impromptu, unofficial campgrounds along the highway and the Walker River. Ten miles or 16 km past Devil's Gate Summit is Huntoon Campground (18 sites, Forest Service). The last three miles to Bridgeport (pop. 500 and 30 miles or 48 km from Walker) are flat. Bridgeport has a somewhat resort-y flavor. When I tried to buy a cube, instead of a pound of margarine, the check-out girl in a supermarket there blew up, citing a county law, etc. She left her post virtually in tears, with me saying, "But I didn't break open a package!" There were a lot of beef cattle and sheep grazing in the area. About 2 miles north of Bridgeport on Hwy. 182 is Paradise Shores Trailer Park adjacent to a lake ($6, swimming).

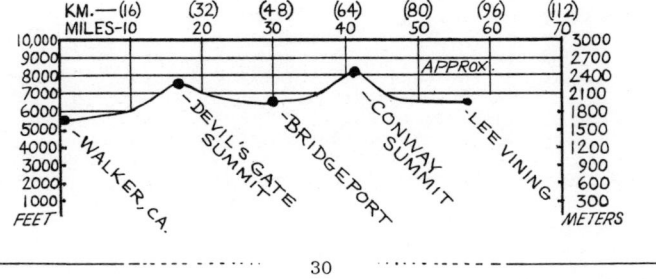

Hwy. 395 after Bridgeport is nice and wide at least to the top of Conway Summit. The downhill has a 6% slope.

Near the intersection of Hwys. 167 and 395 is Mill Creek County Campground, off on Lundy Lake Rd. (50 sites; no fee). Near the north end of Mono Lake is Mono Lake County Park along Hwy. 395 (has piped water). Two cyclists told me they camped there by not setting up their tent till nightfall; I did the same at Gus I. Hess Community Park in Lee Vining (behind the school). It has water, wash basins, and toilets. No one hassled me, though the sprinklers were turned on in half the park all night and I kept waking up thinking that a crew had come to turn on the sprinklers in my part of the park. But the voices I heard were from other campers who came late to the grassy picnic and playground area. I ate at the only restaurant in town, Nicely's, for $7. OK food. The town has a touristy ambience.

Three to 5 miles beyond Lee Vining there are 3 campgrounds off Hwy. 120: Aspen Grove (50 sites; no fee), Big Bend (18 sites; $2 fee), and Lee Vining Creek.

Mono Lake has been in the news lately. There's an information center in Lee Vining run by groups who are trying to preserve the lake, which is shrinking because the city of Los Angeles draws off the lake's tributary waters via aquaducts and tunnels. The lake is highly alkaline and gets more so as its water evaporates. The curious "stalagmites" along the shore are mineral deposits that have been exposed by the lowering water level. And seagulls that breed on islands in the lake are now exposed to predators. The dark island in the center of Mono is actually a volcanic cone. Save Mono Lake!

The Mono Lake "stalagmites".

Yosemite Valley photographed in March from the entrance to the mile-long Wawona tunnel on Highway 41. Bridalveil Falls cascades over the lip of the valley wall. On the left, the sheer face of El Capitan hides

Yosemite Falls, the valley's premier falls. During the summer this view would usually be hazy, but in this photo a winter storm has left the air crisp and clear.

DAY 8

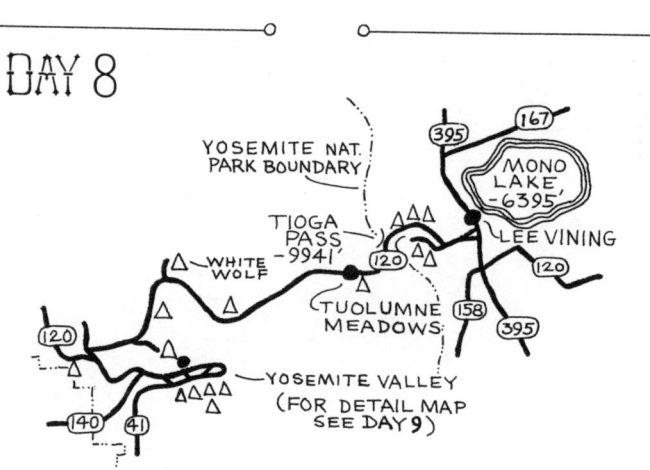

DAY 8. LEE VINING, CA, TO WHITE WOLF CAMPGROUND, YOSEMITE NATIONAL PARK. 44 miles (76 km). Crossing the high Sierra; a tough pass. From Lee Vining it's 12 miles or 19 km to the top of Tioga Pass (the entrance to Yosemite Park) and 75 miles or 120 km to Yosemite Valley. I ended my day's trip at White Wolf Campground above Yosemite Valley because I knew that Yosemite Valley would be crowded (it was a weekend).

From Lee Vining, don't take the first road toward Tioga Pass as you head south--the second road, the "official" Hwy. 120, is less steep. The first several miles of 120 aren't bad; there's even a bike lane--after 3 miles is the turnoff for three campgrounds: Lee Vining Creek, Aspen Grove, and Big Bend; the latter two are several miles off the highway. The climb up Tioga Pass can be tough; I walked my

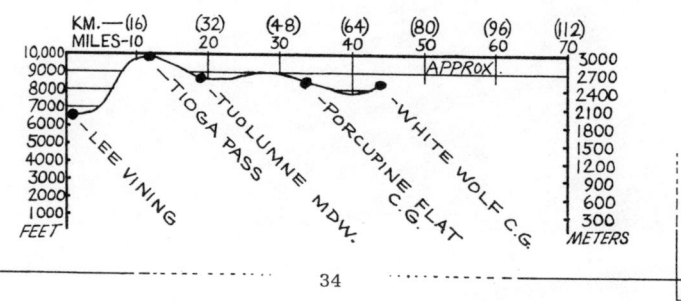

bike part of the time and the thin air made me breathe heavily. Tour buses lumbered by--their exhaust was no help. The first views of snow-covered 10,000-13,000 foot (3,000-3,900 m) peaks are spectacular. Temperatures in September were 60°F or 18°C midway and 48°F or 9°C at the top. I felt glad that I didn't have to climb Conway Summit and Monitor Pass from the eastern side--then they would've been as tough as Climbing Tioga. After the steeper portions of the Tioga Pass road, 10 miles or 16 km from Lee Vining, there's a string of campgrounds: Ellery Lake, Junction (no fee), and Tioga Lake. Also a store (Tioga Pass Resort). If you're bicycling in September or later, stock up on food there--I had to backtrack two miles (drat!) from the park entrance station when I found that there were no food stores open from there all the way to Yosemite Valley.

At the Tioga Pass Entrance Station you'll be provided with all kinds of literature and maps about the park and you'll feel proud to be the only bicycle/s in the line of cars waiting to pay fees. Afterwards, you're in for a 5-mile downhill. 7 miles beyond the entrance station is Tuolumne Meadows (a campground there; its store was closed in September), billed as the largest meadow in the Sierra Nevada. After Tuolumne is some uphill work again--the thin air will cut down on your energy but the scenery is well worth the trouble. The road is on the narrow side, but fortunately no heavy trucks are allowed through Tioga Pass. There's some more uphill work again after Tenaya Lake, another Sierra jewel. 22 miles or 35 km from Tioga Pass is Porcupine Flat Campground; following that is a long downhill glide to Yosemite Creek, the very same creek that cascades down Yosemite Falls in the valley. It's 32 miles or 55 km from Tioga to White Wolf Camp, one mile downhill off the highway.

It was Saturday when I rode into White Wolf Camp--I found it to be chock-full of campers. Cars and monstrous truck-with-travel-trailers were driving around fruitlessly looking for open sites. The lucky campers already there had a superior look as if to say--"Sorry about that, kiddo!" I finally sidled up to a couple just unpacking and asked if I could share their site and got the nod. But the woman became ill and they left for the valley so I became the landlord and folks came up and asked me if they could share the space. One couple who shared my space invited me into their trailer and we had a long chat over dinner. In the morning the temperature was just below freezing.

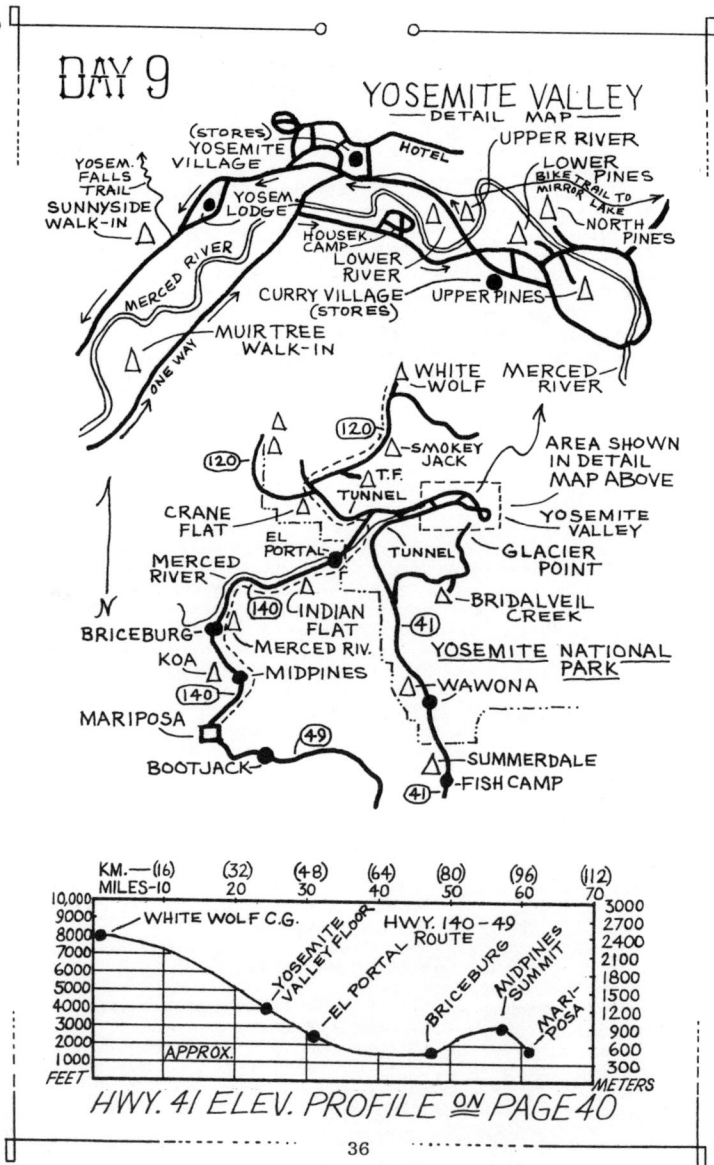

DAY 9. WHITE WOLF CAMPGROUND (YOSEMITE NATIONAL PARK) TO MARIPOSA, CA. 61 miles (98 km). Down into a spectacular glacial valley; and, an alternative.
Six miles or 10 km south of White Wolf Campground on Hwy. 120 is Smokey Jack Campground; 7 miles beyond that is the turnoff for Tamarack Flat Campground, which is about 2 miles off the highway. Riding through this mixed up-and-down area in the early morning, my hands began to freeze. 15 miles or 24 km from White Wolf campground is Crane Flat junction, where you'll turn left and head south toward the valley (nearby is Crane Flat Campground). Then enjoy yourself on a long 9-mile or 15-km coast down to Yosemite Valley, including passage through 2 short tunnels and 1 long tunnel ($\frac{1}{2}$ mile long--I turned my flasher light on). I suggest moving with the speed of traffic if possible, in the middle of the lane, stopping at scenic outlooks if the traffic backs up behind you. Brakes must be in top shape!

On the way down, you'll catch glimpses of the famous Half Dome and the impressive valley walls sculpted by glaciers. The first-time visitor is properly awed. I worked in the valley one summer and explored it then, so on this trip I skipped it. The valley tends to become congested--it even has an occassional smog problem. All of the valley campgrounds require reservations during the summer and early fall. Traffic is such that most valley roads are one-way; several are closed to autos entirely. If you wish to bike the length of the valley (the waterfalls are spectacular) the round trip is 17 miles or 27 km. The detail map on the opposite page gives a fair idea of the layout. There is a bike repair shop in Curry Village. Literature given you at entrance stations will give you a better idea of hiking possibilites, etc.

Once in the valley, I had to decide whether to leave on Hwy. 140 or Hwy. 41. Hwy. 140 is safer and easier (on this day but not the next) while 41 is narrower, less safe, and involves a rigorous climb out of the valley, but it shaves some time off the trip as is more forested and cooler (an altitude profile on the Hwy. 41 route is found on page 42). The fact that I was riding on a weekend, with heavy traffic on 41 (traffic from southern California uses this route) made me choose 140. From the Hwy. 140 junction, it's 7 miles or 11 km along the Merced River (lush scenery) to the little town of El Portal (stores and motels) just beyond the park boundary. Follow 140 down the very picturesque Merced River Canyon (becomes rather arid) to the micro-town of Briceburg ("pop. 9½"), 24 miles or 40 km from the 140 junction. Just before Briceburg is a natural spring on the left. After Briceburg, we leave the Merced River and begin the first work of the day, climbing off and on for 9 miles or 14 km to Midpines Summit. After the first 2 miles of the climb is a curious (and very welcome) little oasis called the Octagon House, run by Julie and Don Skelly, where you can refresh yourself with orange juice or? Just beyond the little town of Midpines are two campgrounds: one is a KOA (private) with swimming pool, groceries and provisions for tent camping. Minimum charge: $7. From Midpines Summit it's a 4-mile coast into Mariposa, a prosperous little city reminiscent of Truckee, except smaller. I stayed at the Sierra View motel in Mariposa ($21.50).

A friendly couple invited me to their house for dinner, even after I told them how great my appetite was. The town is well-blessed with restaurants, motels, a laundromat, etc. Mariposa has a Forest Service office where I went and got some help with my route for several days in advance. The temperature at 4:30 pm was $75°F$. At 7 am the next day, it was $58°F$ (24 and $14°C$).

Julie and Don Skelly in the doorway of their Octagon House.

Highway 49 climbing up to the top of the high ridge between Mariposa and Ahwanee (see page 41).

DAY 10

HWY. 140-49 ROUTE:

HWY. 41 ROUTE:

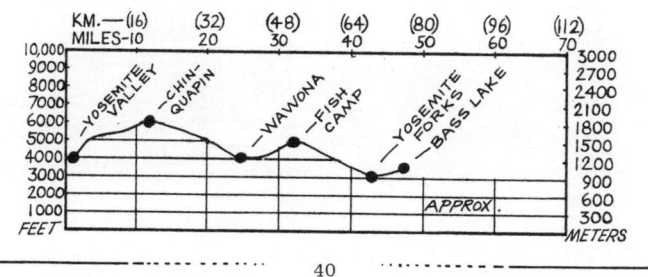

DAY 10. MARIPOSA, CA, TO SPRING COVE CAMPGROUND (BASS LAKE). 37 miles (60 km). Not an easy day.

After a day like this, I began to wish I'd taken Hwy. 41. I got a late start in Mariposa at 11 am. By then the temperature was 80°F (26°C) and rising, at the low elevation of 1950 feet or 585 meters.

After Mariposa on Hwy. 49 is a series of small hills in arid and not especially scenic countryside. In the sun, I began to sweat profusely under my helmet, stopping to cool down and drink from time to time. Mariposa means "butterfly" in Spanish, and sure enough, there were many alongside the highway. Cars knock them out of the air and lizards scurry in the shimmering heat of the asphalt to snap them up.

Eventually I arrived at an impressive scenic overlook where I could see I had some climbing cut out for me. It was a long coast down to a bridge over the Chowchilla River, then an approximately 1,000 foot climb to the top of a ridge which marks the Madera County line, 17 miles or 27 km from Mariposa. At this point the extra-wide road narrows. Then it's downhill through Ahwahnee, which has a grocery store. It's 26 miles or 41 km from Mariposa to Oakhurst, where I made my lunch stop. Oakhurst is a fair-sized town with stores, motels, and a small, shady park next to the town library (water is available there). From Oakhurst, it's a considerable 5-mile climb past residences on Road 426 to the top of a ridge overlooking Bass Lake. I hadn't been aware of this climb when I came to Oakhurst--I assumed that I'd go <u>downhill</u> to get to a lake. But Bass Lake is a man-made reservoir in the hills. Ride downhill a mile or so on the somewhat steep Road 426 to the lake. There is a store at the junction of 426 and 222 which stays open till 6 pm. Luckily, I arrived at 5:50.

All of the popular public campgrounds on Bass Lake are on the western side and reservations during the summer are advised. In mid-September they were mostly closed, except for Spring Cove Campground ($4) which had plenty of excess space. In the fall the lake level is low, leaving some docks high and dry. There are two campgrounds north of (and close by) the 426-222 junction: Denver Church and Forks. South of the junction are, in order: Lupine, Spring Cove, and Wishon Point (the last reportedly has a general store in the summer). Bass Lake has a nice feel--it isn't commercialized. Swimming, boating and hiking are possibilities here.

DAY 11

DAY 11. BASS LAKE TO SHAVER LAKE. 43 miles. From the arid to the verdant; more ups and downs. Today's journey takes us from the relatively dry country of the lower elevations down into a deep river valley and then up a strenuous 5,000-foot (1,500-m) climb to the heavily forested Shaver Lake area.

In late September, the early morning temperature at Bass Lake was 54°F (12°C). In August we recorded a midday temperature there of 105°F (40°C). Cycle south from Bass Lake on Road 222 through pleasant

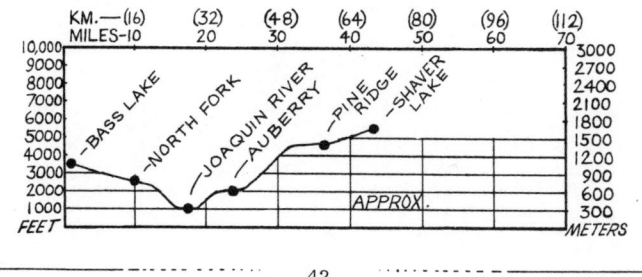

stands of oak, pine and manzanita. About 4 miles south of Wishon, where 222 leaves the lake, turn left on Old Town Road (Road 226), proceed approximately a mile, then turn right on Bonnie 'B' Road (Road 224) and ride about 3 miles to Road 200. Turn left and follow 200 into North Fork, a pleasant, somewhat tourist-oriented town. One of my maps shows a campsite near the town; other sources don't confirm its existence. It's a long, steep, approximately 6-mile coast through arid countryside down to the Joaquin River and PG & E's Wishon Power House. Beyond that, Powerhouse Road can be tough--I was sweating profusely. The top of the grade is reached 4 miles after the river. There are some worthwhile scenic outlooks along the way; my curiosity was piqued by a lemon-y fragrance in the air.

Auberry has a large supermarket. (If you chose not to go the Shaver Lake backcountry route, refer to the maps and comment for Day 12.) I was face-to-face with the limits of my endurance on the serpentine climb out of Auberry on Auberry Road. I felt like I was cycling in the Sahara because the hillside bore directly into the sun and I was hurting under the heat. An alternative is to take the probably-more-gentle-and-wider Highway 168 toward Shaver. However, Auberry Road, once the top of the grade is reached, becomes a rather flat, forested, meandering country road (168 has the traffic).

After Pine Ridge, it's 7 miles or 11 km and a 1,000-foot or 300-m climb to Shaver Lake, sharing the now-twisting and narrow Highway 168 with semis and logging trucks. To get to Dora Belle campground at Shaver Lake turn right on Dorabella St. in Shaver Lake Hts. and ride about one-half mile ($3--in late September the campground was virtually deserted). One mile north of the town is another campground, Camp Edison, while 3 miles out on Dinkey Creek Rd. is Swanson Campground (no piped water). I ate at Angelo's restaurant in Shaver Lake Hts; the meat was tough. SLH has a number of grocery stores and a mountain resort ambience.

After this (for me) especially difficult day, I wrote in my diary: "Why am I _really_ doing this insanity? Sweating and hurting like a religious fanatic while normal people drive cars. Do I want to be apart and special? Do I forget, when I make plans, just how hard it will be?" I dreamed that evening of meeting a former friend who was now in rags because of an alcohol habit. I wondered if I should rescue him.

The old county courthouse in Mariposa.

Above: cowboys herding cattle near Shaver Lake found that a bicycle spooked their cattle; moments later the herd almost trampled the author's parked bike. Below: the isolated road used by the author, cut into the steep canyon wall east of Balch Camp.

DAY 12

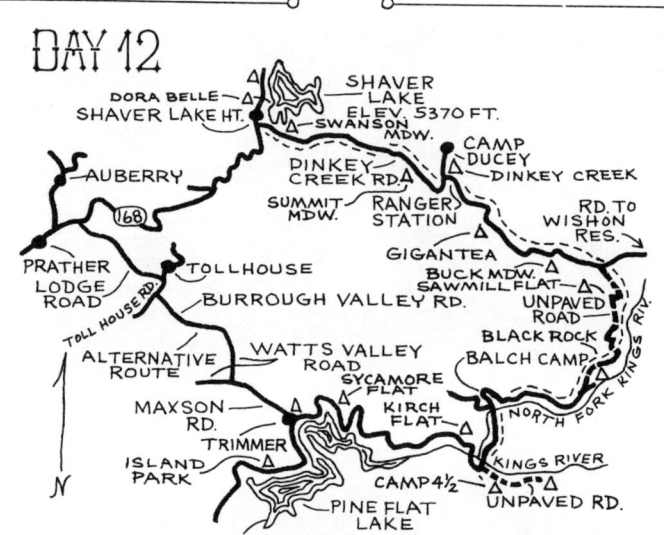

DAY 12. SHAVER LAKE TO CAMP 4½. 50 miles (80 km).
Backroads solitude and beauty, or an easier alternative. I think that the extra mileage and work to go the Shaver Lake-Dinkey Creek high country route is well worth it, considering the cooler temperatures and scenery. The alternative route from Auberry to Pine Flat Lake (see map above) is only 24 miles long and all paved, with gentle hills, but will heat up during the day. Also, the terrain is not Sierra-like, being semi-arid with sparse vegetation.

For my route, take Dinkey Creek Rd. from Hwy. 168 just south of Shaver Lake Hts. and ride 13 miles or 21 km through forested areas to Dinkey Creek Ranger Station (water available). There, turn right on the

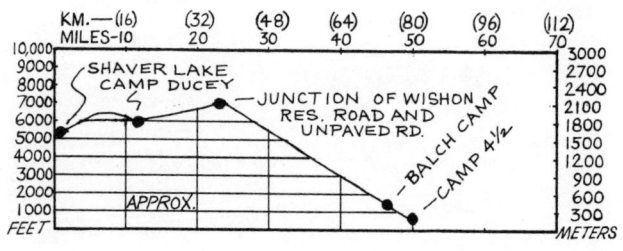

Wishon Reservoir road (well-kept, paved). Five miles from the ranger station is Gigantea Campground (non-piped water available--may have to be purified) and McKinley Grove Picnic Area with impressive giant Sequoia trees. At about 11 miles or 17 km from the Dinkey Creek Ranger Station turn right on an unpaved road marked only by a sign (in 1980) which preaches "pack it in; pack it out" (note: this road may become impassible during heavy rains). The turnoff is about 300 yards or 270 meters before the Tule Meadows Trailer Park turnoff. If you pass over Long Meadow Creek you've gone too far. 1½ miles down this unmarked road you'll pass over the West Fork of Long Meadow Creek (signed). From here on, it's all downhill. The forest was humming with hundreds of hovering yellow bees when I went through--the kind that hang around picnic tables. They're mainly a nuisance, though they can sting if you force them to.

Three miles from Wishon Reservoir road is Sawmill Flat Campground (no piped water--stream water would have to be purified). After this, follow a sign that points to Black Rock Reservoir; here all traces of an old attempt at road paving disappear, but the dirt road is actually smoother. From this point on I only saw one vehicle all the way into Balch Camp. Soon, this road comes out on the edge of the gigantic canyon of the North Fork of the Kings River, with some serpentine downhill bicycling. Be careful of losing your tires' footing on shifty sandy spots. Six miles from Wishon Reservoir road, the coniferous forest gives way to maple trees; later, warm breaths of air from the valleys below replace the cool of the high altitudes. After 10 miles of unpaved road, the paved road begins again, near Black Rock Campground. Now the road, edging downward, is cut into the rock of steep canyon walls and passes under huge penstocks (pipes) carrying water from distant dams to powerhouses below. 21 miles or 34 km from Wishon Reservoir road is Balch Camp, apparently a small company town for power production personnel (didn't see any stores there). With the sun low in the sky, the vistas along the descent through the canyon were spectacular.

A few miles south of Balch Camp, just after the bridge over the main branch of the Kings River, turn left on an unpaved road and proceed a short distance to Camp 4½. There was no one there when I camped, save the resident ranger. I obtained my water from the river. No stores in the immediate area--Trimmer, on Pine Flat Lake, probably has the closest stores.

DAY 13

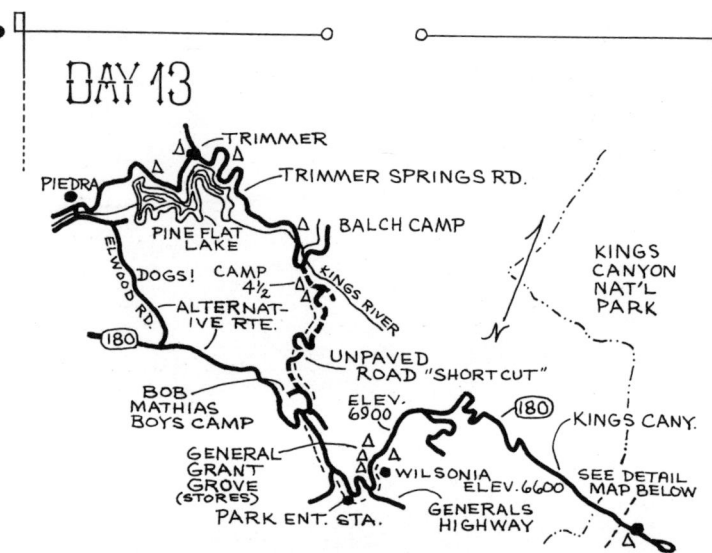

DETAIL MAP • CEDAR GROVE AREA • KINGS CANYON PARK

SHORTCUT + OPTIONAL KINGS CANYON TRIP:

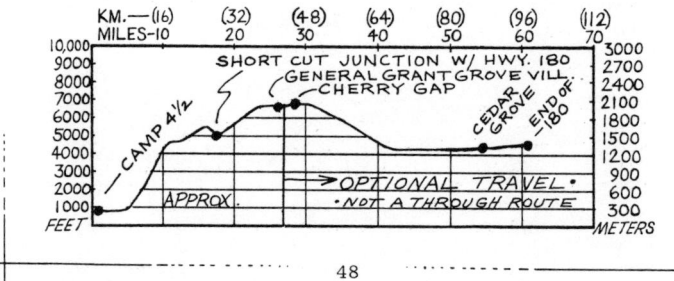

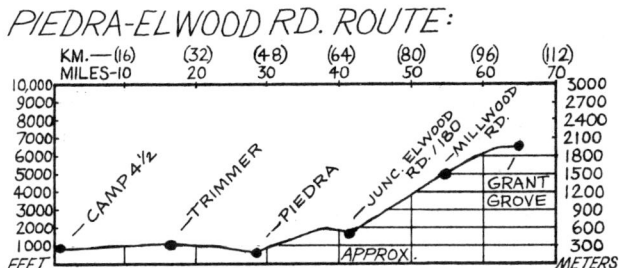

PIEDRA-ELWOOD RD. ROUTE:

DAY 13. CAMP 4½ TO GENERAL GRANT GROVE, KINGS CANYON
NATIONAL PARK. 26 miles (42 km). The roughest day
(and options). The unpaved shortcut I used to get
from Camp 4½ to Hwy. 180 is for the young and plucky
or the old and lucky (the author). It was easily
the roughest, toughest, most trying stretch of my
entire trip. Yet it cut out a lot of miles.

First, let me cover the alternative route (altitude
profile above). It's much longer, but for those
who'd rather not be out in the sticks amid flies--
this route is the answer. Do the low elevation portion as early as possible--the early morning cool
won't last long. Take Trimmer Springs Rd. from Camp
4½ or from Trimmer along the north side of Pine Flat
Lake to Piedra. There are stores in the area. After
Piedra cross the Kings River and head south on Elwood Rd., watching for chasing dogs that are reportedly about halfway to Hwy. 180. Turn left on 180--
about 4 miles up the highway is a store at the junction with Dunlap Rd. Gird yourself for the big
climb--Trimmer Springs and Elwood roads have a few
hills but nothing like this. More info on 180 and
Grant Grove below.

Secondly, I offer some map and altitude profile information on a side excursion into Kings Canyon.
I've hiked, but never biked, in the canyon. If you
want to do this side trip, write for information or
wait and get the excellent brochure at the park
entrance station.

The unpaved shortcut I used would not be passable
during heavy rains. Its sometimes rocky surface
would be hard on delicate tires (I use thick tubes
with my clincher tires). Using the shortcut, the
distance from Camp 4½ to Hwy. 180 is 18 miles or 29
km, but it seems longer. Get as early a start as
possible and take lots of water. To start, head

further east on the road that took you to Camp 4½, passing Camp 4 and arriving, after 2 miles, at a turnoff marked by a sign announcing "Hwy. 180--16 miles". Turn right onto this new road; after a mile or so you'll pass over a concrete water spillway. There are freely grazing cattle and a few houses in the area. The road ascends through the picturesque valleys of Mill Flat and Davis Creeks. About 4 miles from Camp 4½ you'll pass a metal gate. As the road winds upward, trees give way to brush--the hillsides are arid. Ten miles or 16 km from Camp 4½ the road levels off--there's even some downhill riding. Then it's up again. 4 miles beyond the Fox Springs sign one reaches a paved road--turn left here and coast about a mile down to Hwy. 180 on Millwood Rd. From that point it's another 2,000 ft. or 600 m climb to Gen. Grant Grove. There's a gas station along the way with water. Pass through the park entrance station and enter nicely forested areas along the serpentine, narrow highway populated with speeding logging trucks. The Grant Grove portion of Kings Canyon park has four camping areas; several were closed in late September. I camped at Azalea campground ($2) in a tent-only area. Grant Grove Village and Wilsonia are nearby with stores and restaurants.

Here's my hardship story about travelling the shortcut road: I hadn't eaten well at Camp 4½, with no stores in the area. Knowing the shortcut would be tough, I drank my fill of the river and got an early start with 2 water bottles. Along the way, a rancher (who'd never seen anyone bicycle the road) told me about a "Fox Spring, just up the road a few miles." So when I met a ranger driving down the road later, I turned down his offer of water, sure that the spring was close by. After a few more miles, sweating, tired and out of water (no spring), walking the bike and waving away flies that wanted to go up my nose, ears and eyes, I felt less jaunty. Eventually I found a cool creek that crossed the road (7 miles from 4½)--but cows had been in it. I ended up drinking the stuff, even though I didn't have purification tablets. As I became more dehydrated, walking the bike began to tax me--I may have been approaching heat exhaustion--but the insistent flies kept me moving. 14 miles from 4½ I passed the sign pointing to "Fox Springs--½ mi." but I just kept going because I knew I was close to the highway. When I reached it, I found humanity in the form of a cowboy with some beer in his pickup, who gave me a can of the most delicious brew I've had in my life. As for drinking the doubtful creek water, I didn't get sick..... Guess I'm lucky.

The author beginning his trek up Mill Flat Creek Canyon (see previous page).

DAY 14

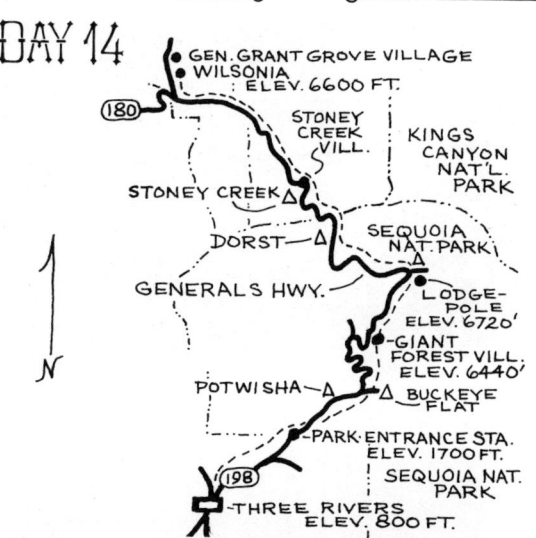

DAY 14. GENERAL GRANT GROVE, KINGS CANYON NATIONAL PARK, TO THREE RIVERS, CA. 52 miles (83 km). Lush forests and another blazing downhill. Today's ride is straightforward, being entirely on Generals Highway and Highway 198, and it's easy, compared to Day 13. I'll primarily cover the campgrounds and visitors' facilities along the route.

When you've recovered sufficiently from Day 13, head southeast on Generals Highway. About 8 miles down the road you'll encounter some gentle hills. At about 12 miles or 19 km is Stoney Creek Village with stores and a restaurant; just down the road is Stoney Creek Campground with piped water ($3 fee). Four miles beyond is Dorst Campground, a large place

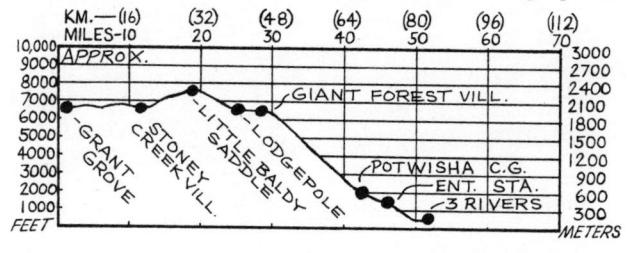

with some 238 combination tent/RV spaces and piped water. My wife and I camped there on our auto trip in August--it was full and dusty; in the early morning semi-tame deer roamed its fringes. 19 miles or 30 km from Grant Grove you'll hit the high altitude for the day at Little Baldy Saddle--7335 ft. or 2200 m. On my trip, just after this point, I encountered a lot of smoke in the air. I learned that forestry crews were doing some "environmental burning"--needless to say, the smoke didn't help my appreciation of nature much. The burning smogged up the entire area. 25 miles or 40 km from Grant Grove is Lodgepole visitor center and camping area (261 sites). The center is modern and attractive; there's a food store and post office. A good place for a rest stop.

29 miles or 46 km from Grant Grove is a larger and older visitors' area--Giant Forest Village--with restaurants, stores and lodging, but no campgrounds. The forest in these areas is rich, with some spectacularly huge trees. From Giant Forest Village the cyclist begins a long descent on switchbacks and long stretches through increasingly arid countryside. The views are impressive. Traffic can be considerable on Generals Highway. 11 miles or 17 km downhill from Giant Forest Village, at 2800 ft. (840 m), is Buckeye Flat Campground, a short way off the highway. About 3 miles beyond is Potwisha Campground. Both are on the small side; both have piped water and a $2 fee. 42 miles or 70 km from Grant Grove is the Ash Mountain entrance station at elev. 1700 ft. (510 m)--also the park headquarters. 10 miles or 16 km beyond is the city of Three Rivers with motels, restaurants and other niceties. Perhaps 7 miles beyond Three Rivers is a campground (Horse Creek Rec. Area) on Lake Kaweah and Hwy. 198.

When I descended down to 1000 feet (300 m) the onslaught of hot air made me feel as though I were in an oven. At 5:30 pm the temperature in the shade at Three Rivers was 93°F. I knew without hesitation that I should cancel the rest of the trip. The next day's travel would've taken me through at least 50 miles or 80 km of below-1000 foot country. I didn't want a repeat of the previous day's shortcut dehydration and discomfort. And besides, I'd covered the rest of the distance to Lake Isabella via car. I checked into the Hill Haven Motel (old and quaint, $15).

I hope to return and ride the last portion of this Sierra route some time. You might wish to ride it if you find the weather agreeable.

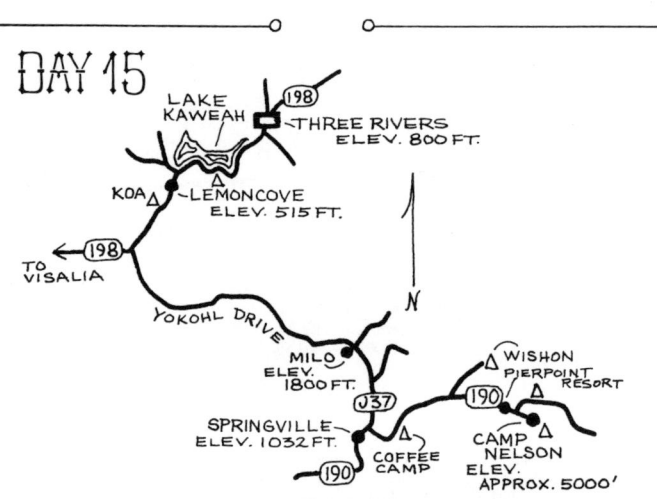

DAY 15. THREE RIVERS, CA, TO CAMP NELSON, CA. 57 miles (91 km). On the flats. I have covered this portion only by car. Start early to avoid the heat. 4 miles from Three Rivers on 198 is a campground--5 mi. beyond is Lemoncove (stores and KOA campground). In August we recorded a not-unusual 100°F here at 3 pm. 7 mi. south of Lemoncove turn left off Hwy. 198 onto Yokohl Dr. (may be known as Mtn. Rd. 296) and bike 22 mi. on the flats to Milo, then another 6 mi. on a narrow road (Hwy. J37 or Hwy. 239) to Springville (stores). There, turn left on Hwy. 190 and start climbing. At 4,400 ft. find Pierpoint Springs Resort--buy food at the store there. At about 5,000 ft. and 18 miles from Springville is Camp Nelson, with 2 restaurants, and nearby Coy Flat Campground (no piped water). Just after Camp Nelson, on 190, is Belknap Campground with piped water.

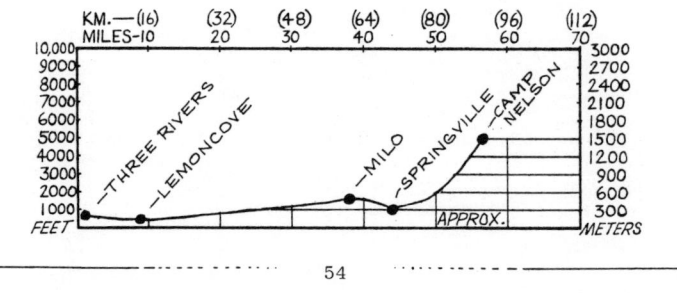

Above: view of west side of Sierra Nevada from the Giant Forest area. Below: the flats and Sierra foothills between Lemon Cove and Springville.

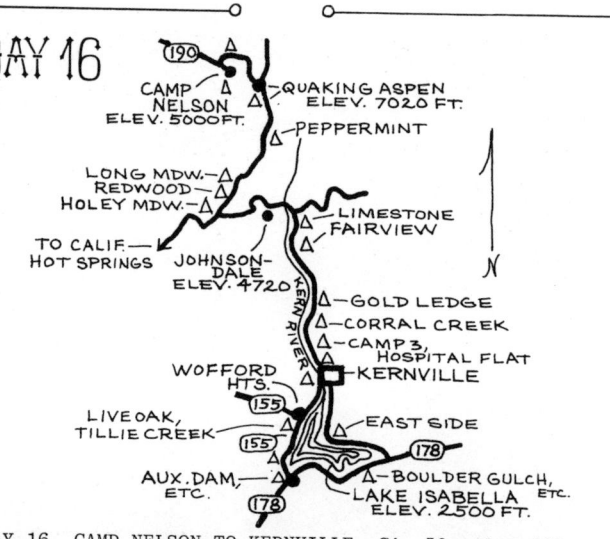

DAY 16. CAMP NELSON TO KERNVILLE, CA. 50 miles (80 km). Coasting down the home stretch. Covered only by car. It's a 2,000 ft. climb and about 10 mi. from Camp Nelson to Quaking Aspen (has store, cafe and campground with piped water). About 6 mi. beyond, on Hwy. 107, is Peppermint Campground (no piped water) --from here it's mostly downhill. Before the Calif. Hot Springs turnoff are 3 campgrounds--all with piped water. Johnsondale, a tired-looking sawmill village, reportedly has a general store. Cross the Kern River and follow it down through its dry picturesque canyon past many campgrounds to Kernville (write for Canyon brochure listed in Resources). Lake Isabella and Kern Canyon are popular with campers and vacationers. The Capri Motel in Wofford Hts. charges $20 for a single and $24 for a double.

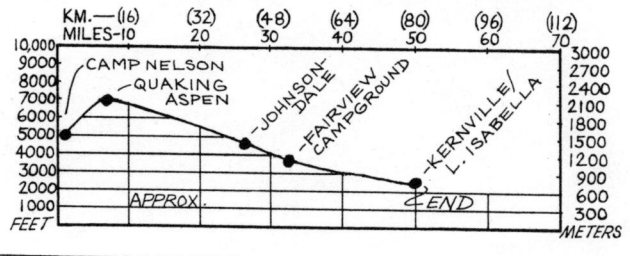

One way to explore the Sierra--work there for a summer. The pair above worked at Lodgepole in Sequoia National Park.

-OTHER SIERRA BIKERS-

Pictured on the front cover: Nick Mayer (his partner, David Spencer, is not shown) of Piedmont, CA, in August, 1980. They had bicycled from Oakland to Lake Tahoe and were returning home via Ebbetts Pass and Bear Valley.

Ralph Mesa of San Jose, CA, pictured near South Lake Tahoe in August. He had ridden from San Jose to Camanche Reservoir via Livermore the first day, to Bear River Reservoir on Hwy. 88 the next, and had reached South Lake Tahoe via Carson Pass the third. Carrying only 20 lbs. of gear, he said that Hwy. 88 was too narrow for good cycling.

John Barsi of La Mesa, CA, pictured on Hwy. 89 near Lake Tahoe in September, had trained in the high altitudes for 2 weeks. This was his first day on a tour that would take him via Hwy. 89 to Mt. Lassen then on to the Oregon border. He planned to return along the Pacific coast and end in San Luis Obispo, carrying 48 lbs. of gear (including a stove) on his Fuji 18-speed which had a low gear of 31 inches.

Ed Wollensack of Chico, CA, got a lift to Truckee, rode down to--and all the way around--Lake Tahoe and was on his way back to Truckee when we met him on Hwy. 267 in August. From Truckee he was catching Hwy. 89 north to Hwy. 70, which would take him most of the way to Chico. He had normal gearing on his 10-speed, said traffic hadn't bothered him and that he was getting the itch for more touring.

Jeff Bergeron (in light-colored shorts) of Colorado and Alex Latzer of New Jersey (both also in the page 2 photo) riding up Luther Pass in September. They met in Yosemite and were riding together as far as Quincy. From there, Jeff (carrying 40 lbs. on a 10-speed) was riding to San Francisco via Eureka. Alex, carrying 60 lbs. on a 15-speed (lowest gear: 30 in.) was riding all the way to Washington state. They said they'd encountered heavy winds around Monitor Pass.

Alistair Smith and Margaret Powell of Kelburn, Wellington, New Zealand, near Devil's Gate Summit in September. Beginning in Fresno, they'd passed through Yosemite and were headed for Lake Tahoe. After that they planned to bike to the Napa Valley, San Francisco, and finally Los Angeles. "You're the first Yank we've seen out here," was their greeting.

Denise Elliott, Michael Teller, and Robert "Speedy" Gonzales in Mariposa in September. They had ridden 116 miles from their homes in the San Jose area to Merced on the first day. On their second day they expected to arrive in Yosemite Valley for a bike rally. They weren't carrying camping gear; had tent reservations in Yosemite.

··PRODUCT EVALUATIONS··

Bellwether small panniers, model 1202, and handlebar bag, model 3001--supplied by manufacturer: I had no equipment failures, stuck zippers or split seams, even though I packed the packs too tightly. Methods for securing the packs to the bike worked well, although I feel that it takes too long to remove the handlebar bag (a problem with all brands). One of the velcro straps on the bag was sewn in backwards but didn't present a problem. I loved the stretch pockets on the sides of the bag. I've used a Bellwether tool bag for a number of years now and it's held up well.

Bellwether cycling shorts--supplied by manufacturer: made of a stretch terrycloth material, these shorts were truly comfortable. I practically lived in them.

Bell "Prime" bicycling helmet--supplied by manufacturer: I was anxious that ventilation in the new "Prime" would not be as good as with their older model, the Biker, since the new helmet doesn't have vent holes. I'll have to confirm my anxiety. The problem is mostly when one is climbing hills in warm temperatures when there's no wind. Sweat literally pours from the helmet. Any helmet using styrene as a liner is going to produce heat build-up. Even the older Biker model (which I've used) has heat build-up but I don't feel that it's as bad. Also, the Biker can be locked to a bike via the vent holes. I would recommend the Biker model for touring purposes, then, or possibly one of the other brands which are partially open on top for ventilation. Both of the Prime helmets sent me had neck strap construction errors--one was too short, the other unusable.

Cycle Guard horizontal flag--supplied by manufacturer: I recommend these safety devices and used one in the Sierra. One caution: the wand can get caught in the spokes if hooked in the secured position while riding. Also, the flag doesn't always hang down the way it should--a wind will cause it to blow back, and it seems to get a permanent backwards curl to it. Maybe they'll improve it. But still, I feel that the Cycle-Guard is better than the whip-antenna type of flag and is better than nothing at all.

Belt Beacon--supplied by manufacturer: I used one on this trip. The beacon worked well, is a good idea, and could be used as an emergency locator.

Ed's Mirror: I'm all for rear-view mirrors, but unfortunately the plastic ball socket on my mirror became enlarged so that the mirror didn't stay stiffly in place and I couldn't use it (maybe I was too rough on it).

The Road Bottle by Rhode Gear: I like the novel bottle holder a lot but feel that the manufacturer didn't use a thick-enough plastic near the neck of the bottle because it buckled when I tried to close the cap on the bottle. Eventually the flexing of the plastic may cause the bottle to crack open.

Grab-On handlebar padding--supplied by manufacturer: I think that thick handlebar padding is the only way to go for touring--though I haven't seen racers use it. The padding eliminated the numb hands I had after long hauls. The competing Cycle-Pro product isn't the same and tends to crack open. After a time, handlebar padding will compress permanently where pressure has been put on it; however, it's possible to rotate the padding to present a fresh surface. I recommend securing Grab-Ons with rubber glue--if just soap is used, the padding will likely slip around if it gets soaked by rain.

Univega Gran Turismo 15 speed bike, 27" frame: worked well; no complaints. As noted, I modified the gears.

Schwinn Le Tour clincher tires: I use them on all long-distance trips. Expensive but worth it.

Huret odometer: seems to be the best odometer system although I had a little trouble with drive belts breaking (some have hairline cracks--take spares).

Tri-Flon lubricant: I used it on my chain with good results. Composed of microscopic beads of Teflon.

Kuban Hitch camera support system (straps that hold a camera against one's chest): didn't work out with my somewhat heavy 35mm camera. I don't think it's designed to be used in a bent-over cycling position. The hitch is really not a quick release system.

Rear bike carriers for cars: don't use them. Rear carriers expose bikes to collision damage and may drag the wheels of larger-frame bikes on the ground when the car hits dips. Bike wheels may stick out beyond the sides of the car, the car's license plate may be obscured, and access to the trunk is made difficult.

··RESOURCES··

Maps

In planning the route I relied much upon AAA maps. They're not always totally accurate, but I found them to be the best quick reference available, and, of course, if you're a member (or have a friend who is and will get them for you), they're free. I used the following AAA maps: <u>Sequoia</u>; <u>Eastern Sierra</u>; <u>Central and Southern California Camping</u>; <u>Feather River and Yuba River Regions</u>; <u>Lake Tahoe Region</u>; <u>Fresno and Kings Counties</u>; <u>Tulare County</u>; <u>Madera, Mariposa and Merced Counties</u>; plus another map (title unknown) which covers Mono Lake to Kings Canyon, with a good detail map of Yosemite Valley. AAA also has <u>CampBook</u>, which lists tent sites in California and Nevada. Most of the above are available from the Automobile Club of Southern Calif., Travel Research and Publications Dept., 2601 S. Figueroa St., Los Angeles, CA 90007, or from the Calif. State Automobile Assn., 150 Van Ness Ave., San Francisco, CA 94102. They seem helpful to cyclists.

A map of <u>Alpine County</u> is available from the Alpine County Chamber of Commerce, Markleeville, CA 96120.

Detailed <u>topographical maps</u> of the Sierra area are available from the U.S. Geological Survey, 555 Battery St., San Francisco, CA. Pertinent maps are 22" x 32" of the Susanville, Chico, Walker Lake, Mariposa, Fresno and Bakersfield areas. I used them frequently when constructing the altitude profiles; however, they're often way out of date as far as roads go.

Books

<u>Bicyclist's Guide To The High Sierra</u> by Norton W. Bell. Available from the author at 1805 Cowper St., Palo Alto, CA 94301. A rather spare book with some loop routes, some non-loop routes and some advice by an experienced Sierra cyclist. $2.95.

<u>Bicycling Through The Mother Lode</u>. Contains 22 tours in the gold rush area of central Calif. (some likely in the Sierra area--I haven't actually seen the book); $3. <u>The American Biking Atlas And Touring Guide</u>, by Sue Browder. Offers 150 tours all over the U.S., 5 of which are in

the Sierra area. $5.95. Both available from Bikecentennial, PO Box 8308, Missoula, MT 59807.

Lassen Volcanic National Park and Yosemite National Park by Jeffrey Schaffer and Sierra Nevada Flora by Norman Weeden published by Wilderness Press, 2440 Bancroft Way, Berkeley, CA 94704. These books stress hiking but also have info of a more general nature about specific regions. All are $9.95 each.

The Mountains Of California by John Muir. An old book by the father of Sierra naturalists; his poetic and occasionally bitter views of the Sierra when it was less developed. Reprinted by Ten Speed Press, PO Box 7123, Berkeley, CA 94707. $5.95.

Brochures and Pamphlets

Guide To The California State Park System. Lists all the state park units and their facilities. $1 from the Distribution Center, Dept. of Parks and Recreation, PO Box 2390, Sacramento, CA 95811.

Campgrounds Of Lake Tahoe. Available free from the Forest Service, Lake Tahoe Basin Management Unit, PO Box 8465, South Lake Tahoe, CA 95731.

Kern River Canyon--A Self-Guided Auto Tour. A well-produced piece showing campgrounds and historical points in the Kern Canyon. Free from the Kernville Ranger Station, PO Box 6, Kernville, CA 93238.

Berkeley To Lake Tahoe Bicycle Touring Guide, free from Nonmotorized Transportation Program, Div. of Transportation Planning, PO Box 214177, Sacramento, CA 94821. Tahoe Bike Routes is free from Caltrans, PO Box 911, Marysville, CA 95901.

Cycle Guide To Yosemite Valley. Write to the Superintendent, Yosemite Nat. Park, CA 95389. Free.

Bikecentennial

Bikecentennial is a non-profit organization totally devoted to serving the touring cyclist. Originally began in the Bicentennial summer of 1976 to help coordinate travel along the newly developed TransAmerica Bicycle Trail, Bikecentennial has expanded along with the sport. It now offers countless services indespensible to the short- and long-distance bike traveller including publications, maps and group trips. Write: Bikecentennial, PO Box 8308, Missoula, MT 59807.

- ABOUT THE AUTHOR -

Bil Paul is married to Lorraine Welch Paul and lives in San Mateo, California. He spends half his work hours working parttime for the Postal Service and half with his photography and book publishing (Alchemist/Light Publishing). His first touring book was Crossing The USA The Short Way: Bicycling A Mississippi River Route, published in 1978 and reprinted in 1980. The guide covers a route from New Orleans to La Crosse, Wisconsin, and the author's experiences in riding it ($3.50). A revision is anticipated.

His other books include The Tri-X Chronicles ($3.45), a photo book of youth in the 1960's, ranging from coverage of GIs in Vietnam to love-ins and student unrest. It's a kaleidoscopic look at a decade which will long be in American memories. A recent book in which Paul combines both his occupations is Mailmen's Dog Stories. He gathered dog stories from letter carriers all over the U.S. and combined 57 of the best into a book that can't be put down. Stories run the gamut of human experience from riotous humor to pathos. $3.95.

Order any of these books from Alchemist/Light Publishing, PO Box 5530, San Francisco, California, 94101. Include $1 additional for mailing (any number of books).